OPEN COURT READING

DATE DUE

NOV 0 4 2011			
JUL 1 1 2019			

T   on

A Division of The McGraw-Hill Companies

Columbus, Ohio

www.sra4kids.com

SRA/McGraw-Hill

*A Division of The **McGraw·Hill** Companies*

Send all inquiries to:
SRA/McGraw-Hill
8787 Orion Place
Columbus, OH 43240-4027

Printed in the United States of America.

ISBN 0-07-572052-3

2 3 4 5 6 7 8 9 QPD 07 06 05 04 03 02

Table of Contents

Unit 5   Courage

Unit 6   Our Country and Its People

SPELLING

▶The *gl, bl,* and *pl* Blends

Visualization Strategy Write the correct spelling for each word. Then use each word in a sentence.

1. plote   plot _____

Answers will vary.
_____

2. glew   glue _____

Answers will vary.
_____

Meaning Strategy Complete each sentence with a word from the box.

plum	blast	blend

3. The loud __blast__ of the fireworks made us jump.

4. Emma bit into the sweet __plum__.

5. __Blend__ the ingredients together slowly.

Name _____ Date _____

▶ Vocabulary Strategies

Read the sentences. Figure out the meaning of each underlined word by looking for a smaller word within it. Write the meaning on the line.

1. When he asked me to give him a million dollars, he said it <u>jokingly</u>.

   in a joking way

2. The movie was so good that it was <u>unforgettable</u>.

   not easy to forget

3. She was <u>joyful</u> when she heard the good news.

   full of joy

4. They <u>modernized</u> our school by adding a computer lab.

   to make modern

5. He <u>repainted</u> the house in green.

   to paint again

6. The dog's <u>bravery</u> saved her life.

   act of being brave

VOCABULARY

GRAMMAR AND USAGE

▶ Common and Proper Nouns

Common nouns *do not* begin with capital letters. **Proper Nouns** *do* begin with capital letters.

▶ **Read the sentences below. Underline the words that should be capitalized.**

1. Declan and <u>james</u> went to <u>washington</u>, <u>d.c.</u> on their vacation.

2. <u>james</u> liked the Washington <u>monument</u>.

3. Declan liked visiting the <u>library</u> of <u>congress</u>.

4. Washington, <u>d.c.</u> is the capital of the <u>united</u> <u>states</u>.

5. Abraham <u>lincoln</u> was the 16th president of the <u>united</u> <u>states</u>.

▶ **Write a sentence using the following proper nouns.**

Answers will vary.

6. Canada _____

7. Jason _____

8. Mississippi River _____

▶Compare and Contrast

Draw pictures of two things you would like to compare. Write the name of each thing. Then, list the ways that they are alike and the ways that they are different.

Answers will vary. Possible answers are shown.

COMPREHENSION

Name: **pencil** _____

Name: **crayon** _____

Ways they are alike: **Both are used to write or draw.** _____

_____

_____

Ways they are different: **Pencils only have one color to**

write. Crayons come in many colors. _____

_____

_____

SPELLING

▶ The *gr, dr,* and *tr* Blends

 Rhyming Strategy Write two words that rhyme with each word below.

1. tree   **possible answers: see and bee**

2. drip   **possible answers: trip and rip**

3. gray   **possible answers: say and day**

4. try   **possible answers: fly and sky**

5. drum   **possible answers: gum and plum**

 Visualization Strategy Write the correct spelling for each word. Then write a sentence using the word.

6. tripp   **trip**

   Answers will vary.

7. graye   **gray**

   Answers will vary.

8. dres   **dress**

   Answers will vary.

▶Context Clues

▶Write the meaning of the underlined word. Read the sentence for context clues to help you.

1. The <u>polar</u> regions are cold areas where some animals live. <u>**cold**</u>

2. <u>Ermines</u> live there and have thick fur, like the other weasels. <u>**weasels**</u>

3. Polar bears also live in <u>arctic</u>, snowy areas. <u>**freezing**</u>

▶Circle the word that has the same meaning as each underlined word.

4. The planets <u>orbit</u> the sun along oval-shaped paths.

   bounce off   (travel around)   pass through

5. The <u>solar</u> system is named for the sun in the center.

   (sun)   star   planet

6. The sun is just one star in a whole <u>galaxy</u> of stars.

   pair   planet   (group)

VOCABULARY

▶Time and Order Words

WRITER'S CRAFT

Time words tell when something happens. Order words tell the order in which things happen.

Read the following paragraph. Circle all of the time words. Underline all of the order words.

Alex wanted to make a poster to get his school to recycle. Before he could start, he had to buy supplies. On Saturday, he went to the store. At the store, he bought poster board and markers. He planned to make his poster on Sunday Finally, he was ready to begin. He wrote why it is good to recycle. First, he wrote that it saves trees. Next, he wrote that it saves animals. Third, he wrote that it cuts down on trash. Then he drew pictures to go with the words. Finally, he was ready to hang his poster in the school.

UNIT I Sharing Stories • **Lesson 2** *Come Back, Jack!*

▶Subject and Object Pronouns

The **subject pronouns** are:
Singular: *I, you, he, she,* and *it*
Plural: *we, you,* and *they*
The **object pronouns** are:
Singular: *me, you, him, her,* and *it*
Plural: *us, you,* and *them*

▶**Fill in the blanks with a correct subject pronoun or object pronoun in the following paragraph.**

Answers may vary.

__We__ went to the Yosemite National Park. __It__ is located in

California. __We__ took our camera with __us__ . __We__ took

pictures of the scenery. __It__ was very beautiful. __I__ think

you should visit __it__ sometime. __We__ had a great time. __We__

walked on trails through the mountains.

▶**Write a sentence using the subject pronoun and object pronoun.**

Answers will vary. Possible answers are shown.

1. *he* and *her* _____

    __He gave a birthday party for her.__

2. *they* and *us* __They brought the cake for us.__

_____

GRAMMAR AND USAGE

SPELLING

▶The Final /k/ Sound

 Consonant-Substitution Strategy Make new words by changing the first letter or letters in each word. Then write a sentence using two of the new words.

1. stack **crack, black, or track**

Answers will vary.

2. book **cook, hook, or took**

Answers will vary.

3. dark **bark, mark, or park**

Answers will vary.

 Proofreading Strategy Circle the five spelling mistakes in the paragraph.

Teaching your dog tricks takes time and hard work. You can read how to do it in a (boock.) Then you can take your dog to the (parck.) You can throw a (stik) and have him bring it to you. You can also (kicke) a ball for him to fetch. You and your dog will have fun learning. Your dog will (barck) with delight.

▶Word Structure

For each underlined word, write the base word. Then write the underlined word's meaning.

1. Justin was <u>fearful</u> about giving the speech.

fear _____

full of fear _____

2. It is <u>dishonest</u> to cheat on a test.

honest _____

not honest _____

3. The party was <u>nonstop</u> fun.

stop _____

not stopping _____

4. Be careful, that vase is <u>breakable</u>.

break _____

able to break _____

5. Our soccer team was <u>unbeaten</u> last year.

beat _____

not beaten _____

VOCABULARY

Name _____ Date _____

▶Action Verbs

GRAMMAR AND USAGE

An **Action Verb** shows what is happening. It also can tell if an action occurred in the past, present, or future.

▶**Use an action verb from the box to complete each sentence.**

revolves	shines	landed	rode	orbits

1. Earth <u>orbits</u> the sun.

2. Earth <u>revolves</u> on its axis.

3. The sun <u>shines</u> during the daytime.

4. Astronauts <u>landed</u> on the moon in 1969.

5. Astronauts <u>rode</u> in a rocket ship to get to the moon.

▶**Write a sentence using the action verb listed.**

6. barks <u>Answers will vary.</u>

7. asks _____

　　　　　Action Verbs • **Challenge**

▶Effective Beginnings and Endings

> A good beginning grabs a reader's attention. It makes readers want to read the rest of the story.
>
> A good ending tells the reader how the story ends.

Write a good beginning and ending for this paragraph.

Answers will vary.

_____

_____

Mr. Fields did not know what to do. He needed the crops. He sold them to stores for money. He used the money to buy food and clothes for his family.

Answers will vary.

_____

_____

▶ Making Inferences

COMPREHENSION

Write a story about a visitor to your school who
is giving a presentation about his or her job.
Decide what job your visitor does for a living.
Give the visitor a name, but do not tell his or her
job. Give clues to let your reader know the
visitor's job. Have another student read your
story and try to figure out your visitor's job.

Stories will vary.

_____

_____

_____

_____

_____

_____

_____

_____

The visitor's job is _____

▶The *nd* and *st* Blends

 Rhyming Strategy Write two words that rhyme with each word below.

1. stand _**possible answers: band and sand**_____

2. just _**possible answers: bust and gust**_____

3. fast _**possible answers: cast and last**_____

4. spend _**possible answers: bend and send**_____

 Visualization Strategy Circle the correct spelling for each word. Then write it on the line.

1. stori	(story)	storee	**story**
2. ponde	ponnd	(pond)	**pond**
3. (hand)	hande	handt	**hand**
4. stuke	(stuck)	stucke	**stuck**
5. losst	loste	(lost)	**lost**

SPELLING

▶Dictionary

▶Look at each pair of guide words. Choose a word from the box that would be found on a dictionary page with each of the guide words. Write the word on the line.

plus	disk	frisk	preset	divert

1. dishcloth/dislike   **disk**

2. plunk/poach   **plus**

3. frill/front   **frisk**

4. dive/divine   **divert**

5. preschool/president   **preset**

▶Write a definition for each word below.   **Answers will vary.**

6. spend   **To pay out money**

7. story   **A telling of events**

8. land   **Solid ground**

▶ Possessive Nouns and Possessive Pronouns

Possessive nouns and **possessive pronouns** are used to show ownership.

Rewrite the sentences using possessive nouns or possessive pronouns. The first one is done for you.

Sentences will vary. Possible answers are shown.

1. The hat of the cowboy was made of straw.

   The cowboy's hat was made of straw.

2. The capital of California is Sacramento.

   California's capital is Sacramento.

3. The book belongs to him.

   It is his book.

4. The ships of Columbus were the Nina, Pinta, and Santa Maria.

   Columbus's ships were the Nina, Pinta, and Santa Maria.

5. The laugh of the hyena sounds unusual.

   The hyena's laugh sounds unusual.

GRAMMAR AND USAGE

WRITER'S CRAFT

▶Staying on Topic

Make sure you stay on your topic when you write. Going off the topic will confuse your reader.

Write details that go with the topic.
Topic: Computers make life easier.

Answers will vary.

_____

_____

_____

_____

Write details that go with the topic.
Topic: We should recycle.

Answers will vary.

_____

_____

_____

_____

▶ Point of View

Write a story about what you did one Saturday.
Use the first-person point of view. On another
piece of paper, rewrite the story using the third-
person point of view.

Stories will vary.

_____

_____

_____

_____

_____

_____

_____

_____

_____

_____

_____

COMPREHENSION

▶Review

 Rhyming Strategy Replace the underlined word in each sentence with a spelling word that rhymes. Make sure the new sentence makes sense.

SPELLING

1. Dad took the dogs for a <u>talk</u>.   walk

2. Her bike got <u>luck</u> in the mud.   stuck

3. The <u>true</u> bird sat on the branch.   blue

4. That dog only knows one <u>pick</u>.   trick

5. The car was going too <u>last</u>.   fast

 Vowel-Substitution Strategy Make new words by changing the underlined vowel in each word.

6. p<u>e</u>st   past, post

7. s<u>o</u>ck   sack, sick, suck

8. bl<u>i</u>nd   bland, blend

9. d<u>e</u>sk   disk, dusk

UNIT 1   Sharing Stories • **Lesson 5** *Tomás and the Library Lady*

▶Thesaurus

▶**For each word below, write another word that means the same thing. Answers will vary.**

1. yell   shout _____

2. thought   idea _____

3. giant   huge _____

4. daring   brave _____

5. error   mistake _____

▶**For each word, write a sentence using another word that means the same thing.**

6. ill   **Answers will vary.** _____

7. slim   **Answers will vary.** _____

8. last   **Answers will vary.** _____

VOCABULARY

Name _____ Date _____

▶Review

Proofread the following paragraphs. Underline three times any letters that should be capitalized. Cross out any possessive noun or pronoun used incorrectly. Write the correct word above it.

                                                     He

Thomas jefferson was president in 1803. ~~Him~~

wanted to purchase some land from france. The

     they

land ~~them~~ owned was on the Mississippi river.

  He

~~Him~~ was able to buy it from king louis of

     It

France. ~~Its~~ was known as the louisiana

Purchase.

    Jefferson'~~s~~ wanted to know more about the

land. He decided that Meriwether lewis and

William Clark should explore it. Lewis and Clark

         They

sailed up the river. ~~Them~~ met many Indians

                           She

along their trip. Sacajawea was one of them. ~~Her~~

          She

was from the shoshone tribe. ~~Her~~ helped guide

    their

them on part of ~~our~~ journey. Lewis and Clark

traveled all the way to the pacific ocean.

Left margin: **GRAMMAR AND USAGE**

▶ Drawing Conclusions

Write riddles about the animals in "Mushroom in the Rain." Trade papers with a partner and have your partner use the information you gave to draw a conclusion about who the character is.

Answers will vary.

Example: I am small and red. I hid under a mushroom when it started to rain. Who am I?

Answer: __an ant__

1. _____

_____

Answer: _____

2. _____

_____

Answer: _____

3. _____

_____

Answer: _____

COMPREHENSION

▶ The /a/ Sound

 **Visualization Strategy** Circle the correct spelling of each word. Then write it on the line.

1. cashe   kash   (cash)   **cash** _____

2. ent   (ant)   int   **ant** _____

3. jamn   jamm   (jam)   **jam** _____

4. (dash)   dashe   dasch   **dash** _____

 Rhyming Strategy Replace the underlined word in each sentence with a spelling word that rhymes. Make sure the sentence makes sense.

5. We walked along the <u>math</u>. **path** _____

6. He <u>pat</u> down when he heard the news. **sat** _____

7. Can you find it on the <u>tap</u>? **map** _____

8. I <u>pad</u> a great time! **had** _____

SPELLING

Name _____ Date _____

 # Base Word Families

▶ Write the base word for each pair below.

1. happily, happiness   <u>happy</u>

2. hoping, hopeful   <u>hope</u>

3. landing, landed   <u>land</u>

4. trusted, trustworthy <u>trust</u>

5. playfulness, playing <u>play</u>

▶ For each word below, write two other words that belong to its family.

6. friend   <u>friendly, friendlier</u>

7. dance   <u>danced, dancing</u>

8. fear   <u>fearful, feared, fearing</u>

9. joy   <u>joyful, joyous</u>

VOCABULARY

MECHANICS

▶Capitalization: Beginnings of Sentences

▶ Read the following paragraph and underline the words that should be capitalized.

<u>jackie</u> Robinson was a baseball player. <u>he</u> was the first African American player in Major League baseball. <u>he</u> was a fantastic player! <u>at</u> the end of his first season he was named Rookie of the Year. <u>later</u> he won the Most Valuable Player award. <u>jackie</u> Robinson is now in the <u>baseball</u> Hall of Fame.

▶ Write two sentences about your favorite athlete, author, or teacher:

1. Answers will vary. _____

_____

2. _____

_____

UNIT 2 Kindness • **Lesson I** *Mushroom in the Rain*

▶Tone of a Personal Letter

In a personal letter, the tone is usually friendly.

Write a personal letter to a friend. Talk about the last book you read. Be sure to use a friendly tone.
Answers will vary.

———————————————————————————————

———————————————————————————————

———————————————————————————————

———————————————————————————————

———————————————————————————————

———————————————————————————————

———————————————————————————————

———————————————————————————————

———————————————————————————————

———————————————————————————————

———————————————————————————————

———————————————————————————————

———————————————————————————————

WRITER'S CRAFT

COMPREHENSION

▶Sequence

Imagine you are on your way home from school one afternoon and you meet some elves. Draw three pictures of things that happen that afternoon. Then, on another piece of paper, write a story telling about the afternoon. The story may include more than just the events you have drawn. Make sure to write things in the correct order of occurrence. **Answers will vary.**

┌───┐
│   │
│   │
│   │
└───┘

┌───┐
│   │
│   │
│   │
└───┘

┌───┐
│   │
│   │
│   │
└───┘

UNIT 2 Kindness • **Lesson 2** *The Elves and the Shoemaker*

▶ The /e/ Sound

 Pronunciation Strategy Say each group of words. Write a spelling word that rhymes. Then write another word with the /e/ sound.

1. net   set   <u>yet</u>   **Answers will vary.**

2. rest   best   <u>nest</u>   **Answers will vary.**

3. dent   rent   <u>went</u>   **Answers will vary.**

4. led   red   <u>fed</u>   **Answers will vary.**

 Proofreading Strategy Circle the three spelling mistakes in the paragraph. Then write the misspelled words correctly.

To ⟨cend⟩ a gift to someone, you need a box, some tape, and a marker. First, wrap the gift and put it in the box. ⟨Thenn⟩, tape the box shut. ⟨Neckst⟩, write your address and your friend's address on the box. Now you are ready to send your package.

send _____

Then _____

Next _____

SPELLING

UNIT 2 Kindness • **Lesson 2** *The Elves and the Shoemaker*

▶Homophones

VOCABULARY

▶Complete each sentence with the correct
homophone pair from the box.

forth	fourth	road	rode
meet	meat	their	they're

1. ___**Meet**___ me at the ___**meat**___ counter for lunch.

2. We went back and ___**forth**___ for the ___**fourth**___ time.

3. ___**They're**___ coming to pick up ___**their**___ new kitten.

4. I ___**rode**___ my bike down the ___**road**___.

▶Write a sentence for each pair of words.

5. hour, our __**Answers will vary.**_____

6. been, bin __**Answers will vary.**_____

7. mist, missed __**Answers will vary.**_____

▶ Commas: Greetings and Closings

Commas are used in the greeting and the closing of a letter.

Read the following letter. It does not have a greeting or a closing. Add a greeting and closing to the letter.

Answers will vary but should contain a comma in the appropriate location.

We are having a great time on our vacation. The weather has been very nice. We have gone to the beach every day. I like to swim in the ocean.

_____

_____

_____

MECHANICS

UNIT 2 Kindness • **Lesson 2** *The Elves and the Shoemaker*

WRITER'S CRAFT

▶Sentence Elaboration

Add more details to your sentences to make your writing better.

Write a sentence or two with details that describe each topic.

1. Your home. **Answers will vary.**
   _____

2. Your pet or a friend's pet. **Answers will vary.**
   _____

3. The sport you like best. **Answers will vary.**
   _____

4. Your school. **Answers will vary.**
   _____

UNIT 2 Kindness • **Lesson 3** *The Paper Crane*

▶The /i/ Sound

Rhyming Strategy Write two words that rhyme with each word below.

1. zip <u>possible answers: lip and rip</u>

2. mix <u>possible answers: fix and six</u>

3. sit <u>possible answers: bit and fit</u>

4. pin <u>possible answers: bin and fin</u>

Consonant-Substitution Strategy Make new words by changing the first letter in each word. Then write a sentence using two of the new words you made.

5. win <u>pin, fin, bin</u>

6. rip <u>lip, hip, zip</u>

7. fix <u>mix or six</u>

<u>Answers will vary.</u>

SPELLING

VOCABULARY

▶ Levels of Specificity Categories

Put each word in the correct category.

Football	Golf	Baseball	Bowling	Raquetball

Sports

	indoor	outdoor
non-team-	raquetball	golf
team-	bowling	football
		baseball

▶Capitalization: Names of Days, Months, and Greetings of Letters

The names of days and months are always capitalized. The greeting of a letter is also capitalized.

Read the following letter. Underline all the words that should be capitalized.

dear Jose,

    I had a great time in school on monday. We learned about the Declaration of Independence. It was signed on july 4, 1776. The declaration of independence was an important part of the American Revolutionary War. The war ended in october 1781 when the British surrendered at Yorktown. I can't wait to learn more on tuesday. We also have to take a test on september 7th. I'll see you at baseball practice on saturday.

    your friend,

Anthony

WRITER'S CRAFT

▶ Structure of a Personal Letter

A personal letter should have a heading, greeting, body, closing, and name.

Write a letter to a friend about something you like to do after school. Make sure you have all the parts.

Answers will vary.
_____

_____

_____

_____

_____

_____

_____

_____

_____

_____

UNIT 2 Kindness • **Lesson 4** *Butterfly House*

▶The /o/ and /aw/ Sounds

 Proofreading Strategy Circle the words that are spelled wrong in each sentence. Then write the misspelled words correctly on the lines.

1. It took a (ling) time to get there. _long_

2. I slept on a (cote) at camp. _cot_

3. Please turn (of) the light. _off_

4. By the lake was a perfect (spat) to set up the tent. _spot_

 Meaning Strategy Write a sentence for each word below.

5. tops __Answers will vary.__

6. flop __Answers will vary.__

7. soft __Answers will vary.__

8. fog __Answers will vary.__

9. drops __Answers will vary.__

SPELLING

▶ Multiple Meanings

VOCABULARY

▶Write two definitions for each word below.

1. duck a bird; to lower _____

2. fly an insect; to move through the air with wings _____

3. punch a drink; to hit _____

4. saw tool; did see _____

▶**Think of another word with two different meanings.**
Write a sentence using each meaning.

Answers will vary. _____

_____

▶Commas: Words in a Series

Commas are used to separate items in a series.

▶**Read the following sentences. Check for the proper use of commas. If a comma is used incorrectly, put an *X* through it. Add any necessary commas. Some sentences do not need commas.**

1. The bread~~,~~ is hard and crusty.

2. The puck flew~~,~~ across the ice,hit my skate, bounced off the pole,and stopped inside the net.

3. Hillary forgot~~,~~ her~~,~~ pencil, paper, and eraser.

4. Althea likes football,soccer,and tennis.

5. We had corn, meatloaf, and potatoes for dinner.

MECHANICS

WRITER'S CRAFT

▶ Time and Order Words

Time words tell when something happens. Order words tell the order in which things happen.

Write a paragraph about things you do on the weekend. Use the time and order words from the box.

second	Sunday	finally	first	Saturday	then

Answers will vary.

_____

_____

_____

_____

_____

_____

_____

_____

_____

_____

_____

▶Making Inferences

Listed below are pairs of people who might have a conversation with each other. Choose one pair and put an *X* beside them. Write a name for each character. Then, think of some ideas about what they might talk about.

Answers will vary.

_____ teacher and student   _____ brother and sister

_____ two best friends   _____ salesperson and customer

Names of characters _____

_____

What might they talk about? _____

_____

On another piece of paper, write a conversation between the characters. Use their names, but never say who they are. Give clues about the characters by what they say. Trade papers with a partner and read each other's conversation. Make an inference about who your partner's characters are.

COMPREHENSION

UNIT 2 Kindness • **Lesson 5** *Corduroy*

▶ The /u/ Sound

SPELLING

 Visualization Strategy Write the correct spelling for each word. Then use each word in a sentence.

1. luk __luck_____

Answers will vary._____

2. muust __must_____

Answers will vary._____

3. rugg __rug_____

Answers will vary._____

 Rhyming Strategy Replace the underlined word in each sentence with a spelling word that rhymes. Make sure the sentence makes sense.

4. The <u>puck</u> quacked loudly. __duck__

5. I like to <u>mug</u> my dog. __hug__

6. Will you come with <u>bus</u>? __us__

7. How <u>such</u> is that game? __much__

The /u/ Sound • Challenge

UNIT 2 Kindness • **Lesson 5** *Corduroy*

▶Homographs

▶**Write a sentence for each word meaning below.**

1. wound- an injury _____ **Answers will vary.** _____

2. wound- wrapped around _____ **Answers will vary.** _____

3. object- a thing _____ **Answers will vary.** _____

4. object- to disagree _____ **Answers will vary.** _____

5. close- near _____ **Answers will vary.** _____

6. close- to shut _____ **Answers will vary.** _____

▶**Think of another homograph and write a sentence for each meaning.**

Answers will vary.

_____

_____

VOCABULARY

► Quotation Marks and Underlining

MECHANICS

Quotation marks are used to identify exact words of a speaker. The first word in a quotation begins with a capital letter. **Underlining** is used for the title of a book or movie.

► **Read the following sentences. Add quotation marks and underlines where necessary.**

1. "The flag is a symbol of our country," said Mrs. Schultz.

2. "The 50 stars are symbols of the 50 states," added Denise.

3. George spoke, "Yes, and the 13 stripes are symbols of the first 13 states."

4. I already knew because I read about it in my book, American History.

5. Doug learned about it in a movie he saw at school called The American Revolution.

6. "Let's all get our book, The Story of America," said Mr. Cho.

▶Sensory Details

Good describing words help readers see, hear, feel, smell, or taste things.

Fill in the blanks with the words in the box.

hot	humid	rough	colorful	sweet

1. Camels live in the __hot_____ desert.

2. Camels have __rough_____ fur.

3. Parrots live in __humid_____ tropical forests.

4. Their feathers are __colorful_____, like a rainbow.

5. When it rains, you can smell the __sweet_____ wildflowers.

WRITER'S CRAFT

UNIT 2 Kindness • **Lesson 6** *The Story of Three Whales*

▶The Final /ən/ Sound

SPELLING

Visualization Strategy Circle the correct spelling for each word. Then write it on the line.

1. wagen   (wagon)   wagin   **wagon**

2. (seven)   sevin   savon   **seven**

3. caben   cabon   (cabin)   **cabin**

4. lemen   lemin   (lemon)   **lemon**

Proofreading Strategy Circle the words that are spelled wrong in each sentence. Then write the misspelled words correctly on the lines.

5. What time does your store (opin)? **open**

6. He is a great (persen) **person**

7. (Chickin) is my favorite food. **chicken**

8. How did this get (brokon)? **broken**

9. The (robon) sang a sweet song. **robin**

UNIT 2 Kindness • **Lesson 6** *The Story of Three Whales*

▶Shades of Meaning

▶Look at the underlined word in each sentence. Choose a word from the box that makes the meaning of the word clearer. Write the word on the line.

| thrilled   loads   spotless   thunderous   terrified |

1. The crowd's <u>loud</u> laughter filled the theater.

   <u>thunderous</u>

2. His room was <u>clean</u>. <u>spotless</u>

3. She was <u>happy</u> when her friends threw her a party.

   <u>thrilled</u>

4. The <u>scared</u> cat ran under the bed when she heard the

   thunder. <u>terrified</u>

5. We made <u>lots</u> of money at the bake sale. <u>loads</u>

▶Think of a more meaningful word that means the same as each word below. Use each word in a sentence.

6. hot <u>**Answers will vary.**</u>

7. mad <u>**Answers will vary.**</u>

VOCABULARY

UNIT 2 Kindness • **Lesson 6** *The Story of Three Whales*

▶ Commas: Cities, States, and Dates

MECHANICS

Commas are used between a city and a state. Commas are also used between the day and the year when writing a date.

▶ **Read the following sentences. Add any commas that are necessary. Put an *X* on any comma that is used incorrectly.**

1. Lucy lives in Topeka,Kansas.

2. She went to visit her cousin on May 30,2000.

3. Her cousin lives in Gettysburg,Pennsylvania.

4. A famous Civil‚Ⅹ War battle was fought at Gettysburg.

5. The battle of Gettysburg‚Ⅹ started on July 1,1863.

6. President Lincoln gave a famous speech at Gettysburg on November 19,1863.

▶ Structure of a Business Letter

A business letter should have a heading, inside address, greeting, body, closing, and name.

Write a letter to a company asking for donations. Make sure you have all the parts.

Answers will vary.

_____

_____

_____

_____

_____

_____

_____

_____

_____

_____

WRITER'S CRAFT

▶Review

Consonant-Substitution Strategy Make new words by changing the first letter in each word. Then write a sentence using two of the new words you made.

SPELLING

1. rush **gush, hush, mush** _____

2. bend **lend, send** _____

3. got **dot, hot, pot, lot, not, spot** _____

4. west **best, nest, rest, zest, pest** _____

Answers will vary. _____

Rhyming Strategy Replace the underlined word in each sentence with a spelling word that rhymes. Make sure the sentence makes sense.

5. Clean with those <u>bags</u>. **rags** _____

6. Let's have some cookies and <u>silk</u>. **milk** _____

7. I <u>shove</u> my rabbit. **love** _____

8. Would you put another <u>clog</u> on the fire? **log** _____

Name _____ Date _____

▶Review

▶Complete each sentence with a word from the box.

| tail | bin | week | been | tale | weak |

VOCABULARY

1. Last __week__ we had a test on the United States.

2. The dog's __tail__ got caught in the door.

3. I felt so __weak__ when I had the flu.

4. Please put your toys in the __bin__.

5. Our teacher read us a __tale__ about a powerful princess.

6. How have you __been__ feeling?

▶Write another definition for each word.

7. present- a gift __to give__

8. desert- to leave __dry land__

9. wind- air __to turn__

UNIT 2 Kindness • **Lesson 7** *Cinderella*

▶Review

MECHANICS

Remember the rules for **commas, capital letters, and quotation marks.**

▶ **Read the following paragraph. Underline any word that should be capitalized. Add quotation marks, underlines, and commas where they should be.**

Joaquin will be 12 on <u>friday</u>, <u>march</u> 15,2002. <u>he</u> wants a telescope,a telescope stand,and the book <u>Astronomy</u> for his birthday. <u>with</u> a telescope he will be able to see planets like Mars,Saturn,and maybe Pluto. <u>his</u> birthday party will be on <u>saturday</u>, <u>march</u> 16,2002. <u>his</u> party is going to be at his house in <u>san</u> <u>antonio</u>,Texas. Joaquin is going to write letters to invite his friends to his birthday party.

▶ **Write a letter for Joaquin to invite a friend to his birthday party. Remember to use correct punctuation.**

Dear _____,

_____

_____

Sincerely,

Joaquin

Name _____ Date _____

▶Background Information

Background information about people, places, and events.

Write a note to your friend explaining why you cannot come to the party this weekend.

Answers will vary.

_____

_____

_____

_____

UNIT 3 Look Again • **Lesson 1** *I See Animals Hiding*

►The /ā/ Sound

Rhyming Strategy Replace the underlined word in each sentence with a spelling word that rhymes. Make sure the sentence makes sense.

1. Pour the water into the <u>snail</u>. **pail** ____

2. Please <u>bait</u> for me. **wait** ____

3. Is that diamond real or <u>cake</u>? **fake** ____

4. Which <u>ray</u> does it go? **way** ____

Visualization Strategy Circle the four spelling mistakes in the paragraph. Then write the misspelled words correctly on the lines.

If you are ever walking along a (trale) and see a

(snak), don't go near it. Even though some

snakes are not dangerous, it is best to be (saif)

(Stae) away from snakes!

5. **trail** ____   7. **safe** ____

6. **snake** ____   8. **stay** ____

▶Base Word Families

▶Add prefixes and suffixes to the words below to make new words in the base word family.   **Answers will vary.**

1. write   **rewrite, writing**

2. forgive   **forgiving, forgiveness**

3. type   **typing, typed, retype**

4. happy   **happiness, unhappy**

▶Write another word in the base word family for each word. Then use the word in a sentence.

5. quietness **Answers will vary.**

_____

6. joke   **Answers will vary.**

_____

VOCABULARY

▶ Sentences and End Marks

Remember there are four kinds of sentences: **declarative**, **interrogative**, **imperative**, and **exclamatory**. Remember the punctuation for each kind of sentence.

▶ **Read each sentence. Write what kind of sentence it is on the line. Also, put a period, question mark, or an exclamation mark at the end of the sentence.**

1. The frog jumped from the pond to the log. <u>declarative</u>

2. Can a toad jump? <u>interrogative</u>

3. Wow, that toad jumped really high! <u>exclamatory</u>

4. How high did that toad jump? <u>interrogative</u>

5. Please go to the pond. <u>imperative</u>

▶ **Rewrite the declarative sentence as an interrogative sentence.**

6. We don't have to go to school on Friday.

   Do we have to go to school on Friday?

7. Todd is going to baseball practice after school.

   Is Todd going to baseball practice after school?

▶Expository Structure

Expository writing gives facts.

- ▶ Put the most important facts first.

- ▶ List details in the order in which things happen.

Think of a story you just heard. Write a paragraph telling about the event.

Answers will vary.

_____

_____

_____

_____

_____

WRITER'S CRAFT

WRITER'S CRAFT

▶Topic Sentences

A topic sentence tells about the paragraph. It is often the first sentence of a paragraph.

Think of something you learned about nature. Write a topic sentence and three details about it.

Answers will vary.

_____

_____

_____

_____

_____

_____

▶ Drawing Conclusions

Write a paragraph about an animal that you like. Give some clues about the animal, but don't tell what the animal is. Trade papers with a partner. Have them draw a conclusion about what animal the paragraph is about and also tell what the clues were.   **Answers will vary.**

COMPREHENSION

_____

_____

_____

_____

_____

_____

What is the animal? _____

_____

How do you know? _____

_____

_____

UNIT 3 • Look Again • **Lesson 2** *They Thought They Saw Him*

▶ The /ē/ Sound

Visualization Strategy Circle the correct spelling for each word. Then write it on the line.

SPELLING

1. thease   theese   (these)   **these**

2. grean   (green)   grene   **green**

3. dreem   dreme   (dream)   **dream**

4. (leaves)   leeves   leves   **leaves**

5. happee   (happy)   happey   **happy**

Pronunciation Strategy Read each sentence. Circle the words that have the /ē/ sound.

6. The soccer (team) had sore (feet)

7. You should never (sneak) up on someone.

8. I had a (silly) (dream) last night.

9. Give (each) player a turn.

Name _____ Date _____

 # Prefixes

▶ Add the prefixes *over-* or *un-* to each word to make a new word. Use each word in a sentence.

1. fill   <u>overfill, Answers will vary</u>

2. common   <u>uncommon, Answers will vary</u>

3. board   <u>overboard, Answers will vary</u>

4. lap   <u>overlap, Answers will vary</u>

5. easy   <u>uneasy, Answers will vary</u>

6. kind   <u>unkind, Answers will vary</u>

▶ Think of two more words that start with *over-* and *un-*. Use them in a sentence.

<u>Answers will vary.</u>

_____

VOCABULARY

▶ GRAMMAR AND USAGE

▶ Linking Verbs and Helping Verbs

Linking verbs are used to help connect or join parts of a sentence. Helping verbs are used with action verbs to tell when something has happened.

▶ **Fill in the blanks with a linking or helping verb. Write** *helping* **or** *linking* **on the line.** **Answers may vary. Possible answers shown.**

1. Amelia Bedelia <u>is</u> a funny book. <u>linking</u>

2. Amelia Bedelia <u>was</u> written by Peggy Parish. <u>helping</u>

3. My favorite book <u>is</u> Treasure Island. <u>linking</u>

4. I <u>am</u> going to read many books this summer. <u>helping</u>

▶ **Underline the linking or helping verb in each sentence. Write** *helping* **or** *linking* **on the line.**

5. The Nile River <u>is</u> in Egypt. <u>linking</u>

6. Egypt <u>is</u> on the continent of Africa. <u>linking</u>

7. The pyramids <u>were</u> built in Egypt. <u>helping</u>

8. King Tut <u>was</u> an Egyptian king. <u>linking</u>

▶Note Taking

Taking good notes helps you remember facts. Write down only the most important facts.

Read the paragraph below. Write notes about this paragraph.

Golden retrievers are dogs that have gold fur. They are about 22 inches tall. They usually weigh about 65 pounds. Golden retrievers are popular pets. They are gentle and loving. They are also playful.

<u>Golden Retrievers</u>

22 inches tall
_____

65 pounds
_____

gentle and loving
_____

_____

_____

_____

_____

WRITER'S CRAFT

UNIT 3 Look Again • **Lesson 3** *Hungry Little Hare*

▶The /ī/ Sound

Rhyming Strategy Choose a word from the box that rhymes with each word below. Then use the word in a sentence.

fly	night	find

SPELLING

1. cry ^fly _____
   <u>Answers will vary.</u> _____

2. kind ^find _____
   <u>Answers will vary.</u> _____

3. light ^night _____
   <u>Answers will vary.</u> _____

Proofreading Strategy Circle the words that are spelled wrong. Then write the misspelled words correctly.

4. My dad makes the best cherry (pi). ^pie _____

5. You can put your coat (rite) here. ^right _____

6. That movie made me (crie). ^cry _____

7. Please turn out the (lite). ^light _____

►Compound Words

►Add a second word to each word below to make a compound word. Write the new word on the line.

1. sun __Answers will vary.__

2. fire __Answers will vary.__

3. ball __Answers will vary.__

4. house __Answers will vary.__

5. rain __Answers will vary.__

►Make a compound word to complete each sentence.

6. Aaron played base __ball__ at the park today.

7. The sun __light or shine__ was in our eyes.

8. The play __ground__ was crowded.

9. We had to leave early because of a

thunder __storm__.

VOCABULARY

UNIT 3 Look Again • **Lesson 3** *Hungry Little Hare*

▶ Subject/Verb Agreement

The subject and verb of a sentence must agree.

▶**Fill in the blank with the correct verb tense.**

1. The bird __flies__ in the air. (fly)

2. An owl __hoots__. (hoot)

3. The frog __leaps__ on the lily pad. (leap)

▶**Fill in the blank with the correct verb tense.**

4. Bats __fly__ at night. (fly)

5. The elephants __walk__ in the jungle. (walk)

UNIT 3   Look Again • **Lesson 3** *Hungry Little Hare*

▶Transition Words

Transition words show **time** and **order**.

Think of the things you do when you get home from school. Write a paragraph telling about them using transition words.

Answers will vary.

_____

_____

_____

_____

WRITER'S CRAFT

▶The /ō/ Sound

 Consonant-Substitution Strategy Change the underlined letter or letters to make two new rhyming words.

1. <u>bl</u>ow _____ **Possible answers: bow, throw, or row.**

2. <u>b</u>oat _____ **Possible answers: float, coat, or moat.**

3. <u>p</u>oke _____ **Possible answers: smoke or joke.**

 Meaning Strategy Write a sentence for each word below.

4. show **Answers will vary.**

5. slowly **Answers will vary.**

6. note **Answers will vary.**

7. soap **Answers will vary.**

8. over **Answers will vary.**

▶Suffixes

▶**Fill in the blank with *-er* or *-est*.**

1. Who is the tall **er**___ person, Janie or Rosie?

2. Retrievers are one of the smart **est**___ breeds of dogs.

3. That is the long **est**___ slide I have ever seen!

4. Today is much cold **er**___ than yesterday.

5. The cake tastes sweet **er**___ than the ice cream.

▶**Write a sentence that compares each of the people or things below.**   **Answers will vary.**

6. Your best friend and you

   _____

7. Your two favorite animals

   _____

8. Spelling and math

   _____

VOCABULARY

▶ Parts of a Sentence

A sentence contains a **subject** and a **predicate**. The subject tells who or what the sentence is about. The predicate tells what the subject *is* or *does*.

▶**Draw a line under the subject and circle the predicate.**

1. Fossils are evidence that an animal or plant once lived.

2. Fossils are formed over many years.

3. An animal or plant dies and is buried.

4. Layers of rock build up on the plant or animal over millions of years.

5. The hardest part of the animal or plant hardens into fossils.

6. Some rock layers get pushed up closer to the surface of the earth.

7. Scientists find the buried fossils by digging in these rock layers.

GRAMMAR AND USAGE

▶Organizing Expository Writing

Expository writing gives facts.

> ▶ Put the most important facts first.

> ▶ List details in the order in which things happen.

Think about how to make a sandwich. Write a paragraph telling how to do it.

Answers will vary.

_____

_____

_____

_____

_____

WRITER'S CRAFT

▶ Supporting Details

WRITER'S CRAFT

Supporting details tell about the main idea.

Write a paragraph about the main idea below. Use at least three details to support the main idea.

Main Idea: Ways we can help the elderly in our community.

Answers will vary.

_____

_____

_____

_____

_____

▶Classifying and Categorizing

On the lines below, write as many different animals as you can think of. Then, think of categories that at least one of the animals could fit into. Write three of the categories on this paper and list the animals that fit each category. **Answers will vary.**

_____ _____ _____

_____ _____ _____

_____ _____ _____

Category 1: _____

Animals: _____

_____

Category 2: _____

Animals: _____

_____

Category 3: _____

Animals: _____

_____

COMPREHENSION

UNIT 3 **Look Again** • **Lesson 5** *How the Guinea Fowl Got Her Spots*

▶The /o͞o/ Sound

Visualization Strategy Circle the correct spelling for each word. Then write it on the line.

1. fude   fewd   fud   (food)   food

2. (tune)   tun   toon   tewn   tune

3. nue   nuw   (new)   noo   new

Vowel-Substitution Strategy Fill in the blanks with the correct letters that spell each word.

4. The m oo n has a dusty surface.

5. Wh o is that girl?

6. It's r u d e to yell at people.

7. D o you know how to get there?

8. Is there r oo m for one more?

SPELLING

▶Suffixes

▶**Add *-ing* or *-ly* to each underlined word.**

1. He is always <u>talk **ing**</u> on the phone.

2. They were a <u>live **ly**</u> group.

3. They jumped up and down <u>joyful **ly**</u>.

4. She is <u>visit **ing**</u> her cousin in Maine.

▶**Follow the directions next to each number. Write a word ending in *-ing* or *-ly*.**

5. Describe what someone in a play is doing now.

   word ending in *-ing*, Answers will vary

6. Describe how someone is running.

   word ending in *-ly*, Answers will vary

7. Describe what you are doing now.

   word ending in *-ing*, Answers will vary

VOCABULARY

GRAMMAR AND USAGE

▶Complete Sentences

A complete sentence expresses a thought and contains a subject and predicate.

Read the following sentences. Mark them as *C* for a complete sentence, *R* for a run-on sentence, or *F* for a sentence fragment. If the sentence is a fragment or a run-on, then rewrite it correctly on the line.

1. Dublin is the capital of Ireland. __C__

_____

2. The island of Ireland. __F__

The island of Ireland is in the Atlantic Ocean.

Answers will vary.

3. Finn MacCool is an Irish folk tale hero he did many great things for Ireland. __R__

Finn MacCool is an Irish folk tale hero. He did many great

things for Ireland.

4. It rains often in Ireland. __C__

_____

▶Place and Location Words

Place and **location words** tell where things are located.

Pretend it is your job to show a new student around your school. Write sentences telling the student where things are in the school.

Answers will vary.

_____

_____

_____

_____

_____

WRITER'S CRAFT

COMPREHENSION

▶ Main Idea and Details

Suppose you could camouflage yourself anytime you wanted to. Why would you do it? When and how would you do it? Complete the main-idea sentence below. Then, finish the paragraph by writing detail sentences.   **Answers will vary.**

Main-idea Sentence:

If I could camouflage myself, I would _____

_____

_____

Detail Sentences:

_____

_____

_____

_____

_____

_____

_____

_____

▶Review

Proofreading Strategy Circle the five spelling mistakes in the paragraph. Then write the misspelled words correctly on the lines.

If you ever visit the (deap) sea, you just (mite) see a

seal. Most (seels) live in polar areas, where there

is (snoe). Seals enjoy a (meel) of fish. They are fun

to watch.

1. **deep**

2. **might**

3. **seals**

4. **snow**

5. **meal**

Visualization Strategy Write the spelling word with the same vowel spelling as each set of words.

6. leak   peak   **weak**

7. bake   take   **rake**

8. dune   tune   **costume**

9. thy   why   **shy**

SPELLING

Name _____ Date _____

►Review

►Complete each sentence by adding a prefix or suffix from the box to each underlined word. Then write the word.

over-	un-	-er	-est	-ing	-ly

1. Alaska is cold<u>er</u> than Hawaii. **colder**

2. If you work hard, you can <u>over</u>come anything.

overcome

3. I like pick<u>ing</u> apples. **picking**

4. Throw away any <u>un</u>used parts. **unused**

5. He smiled warm<u>ly</u>. **warmly**

6. That is the bright<u>est</u> shirt I have ever seen!

brightest

►Write a sentence using two compound words. **Answers will vary.**

_____

_____

VOCABULARY

Name _____ Date _____

▶Review

▶Read the sentence. Write what kind of sentence it is on the line. Underline the subject and circle the predicate.

1. The United States (has five Great Lakes.)

   declarative _____

▶Read the sentence. Write *run-on sentence* or *sentence fragment* on the line. Rewrite the sentence correctly.

2. The five Great Lakes border Canada and the United States I go to Lake Huron every summer. run-on sentence

   The five Great Lakes border Canada and the United

   States. I go to Lake Huron every summer.

▶Underline the helping or linking verbs. Write *helping* or *linking* on the line.

3. Lake Ontario is the smallest Great Lake. linking

4. The Great Lakes were formed many years ago. helping

GRAMMAR AND USAGE

WRITER'S CRAFT

▶ Fact and Opinion

> ▶ A **fact** is something true.

> ▶ An **opinion** is a person's idea.

Think of an animal you like. Write both facts and opinions about the animal below.

Animal: Answers will vary. _____

Facts: Answers will vary. _____

_____

_____

_____

_____

Opinions: Answers will vary. _____

_____

_____

_____

_____

UNIT 4 Fossils • **Lesson I** *Fossils Tell of Long Ago*

▶ Words with *wh* and *sh*

 Meaning Strategy Add *wh* or *sh* to each word to complete the sentence.

1. __wh__y did the car stop running?

2. We saw a fla__sh__ of light.

3. Wait here __wh__ile I get your coat.

4. Can you tell me __wh__ere the mall is?

5. The boot washed up on the __sh__ore.

 Visualization Strategy Circle the correct spelling for each word. Then write it on the line.

6. frech   fresch   (fresh)   **fresh** _____

7. schine   (shine)   chine   **shine** _____

8. wen   (when)   whene   **when** _____

9. clach   clasch   (clash)   **clash** _____

SPELLING

▶Concept Words

Read the paragraph and answer the questions that follow.

It is important for everyone to recycle. It helps the environment when we reuse things instead of throwing them away. We can reuse paper products, plastic, and glass. Reusing paper products saves trees and animals. When we cut down trees for paper, we hurt the animals that need the trees.

1. What is the concept of recycling?

To reuse things _____

2. What context clue tells you about the meaning of recycling?

The word "reuse" _____

►Adjectives

Adjectives are words used to describe nouns.

►**Write an adjective to complete each sentence.**

Answers will vary.

1. The _____ rabbit caused the trouble.

2. The sun is _____.

3. Juan rode his _____ bike.

4. Manuel needed a _____ jacket.

5. The _____ puppy wanted to sit in my lap.

6. Kevin baked _____ bread.

►**Write an adjective for each noun and use the words in a sentence.** **Answers will vary.**

7. _____ clown

_____

_____

8. _____ horse

_____

_____

GRAMMAR AND USAGE

▶ Fact and Opinion

▶ From "The Dinosaur Who Lived in My Backyard," you learned that you can compare the size of dinosaurs to many interesting things. Imagine that you are a dinosaur. You are living in someone's backyard. From the point of view of the dinosaur, write two sentences that compare your size to the size of the people. **Answers will vary.**

_____

_____

_____

_____

▶ Now, from the dinosaur's point of view again, write two sentences that are your opinion about the size of the people. **Answers will vary.**

_____

_____

_____

_____

COMPREHENSION

▶ Words with *ch* and *th*

 Consonant Substitution Add *ch* and *th* to each word below to make two new words. Write the words on the lines.

1. ick _____   <u>**chick and thick**</u>

2. in _____   <u>**chin, inch, or thin**</u>

 Rhyming Strategy Replace the underlined word in each sentence with a spelling word that rhymes. Make sure the sentence makes sense.

Answers will vary.

3. What did they <u>peach</u> you in school today?

<u>**teach**</u>

4. When the egg <u>batched</u>, a baby bird appeared.

<u>**hatched**</u>

5. Be careful not to <u>broke</u> on that candy.

<u>**choke**</u>

6. Ask your <u>other</u> to call me.

<u>**mother**</u>

SPELLING

▶Synonyms

VOCABULARY

▶**Write a word on the line that is a synonym for each underlined word.** **Answers will vary.**

1. He <u>called</u> my name across the field. _shouted, yelled_

2. A <u>thief</u> stole my wallet! _robber, burglar, crook_

3. Zack <u>injured</u> his leg when he fell. _hurt, wounded_

4. The cafeteria is <u>below</u> the library. _beneath, under_

▶**Write two words that mean the same as each word below.** **Answers will vary.**

5. glad _happy, pleased, joyful_

6. large _big, huge_

7. weep _cry, sob, bawl_

8. stumble _fall, trip, slip_

UNIT 4 Fossils • **Lesson 2** *The Dinosaur Who Lived in My Backyard*

▶ Contractions

A contraction is a shortened form of two words that are joined together. An apostrophe (') takes the place of the missing letter or letters.

▶ **Read the pair of words. Write a contraction on the line.**

1. I will   I'll _____

2. do not   don't _____

3. it is   it's _____

▶ **Rewrite each sentence. Use a contraction in place of the underlined words.**

4. <u>I have</u> read this book three times.

   I've read this book three times. _____

5. <u>You are</u> a good friend.

   You're a good friend. _____

6. The doctor said <u>I will</u> feel better tomorrow.

   The doctor said I'll feel better tomorrow. _____

GRAMMAR AND USAGE

▶Rhyme

WRITER'S CRAFT

In **rhyming** poetry, the last word in a line rhymes
with the last word in another line.

**Think of someone that is special to you.
Write a rhyming poem about your feelings.**

Answers will vary.

_____

_____

_____

_____

_____

_____

_____

▶Classifying and Categorizing

Look at the words in the box below. They fit into two categories. Each category is the name of a room in a house. Fit the words into the blanks so that the letters in the box give the name of a room. Use one space for each letter.

bed	sink	stove	dresser
mirror	oven	lamp	clock
microwave	bookcase	dishes	mixer
desk	potholder		

COMPREHENSION

UNIT 4 Fossils • **Lesson 3** *Dinosaur Fossils*

▶The /ar/ Sound

SPELLING

Rhyming Strategy Write two words that rhyme with each word below. **Answers may vary.**

1. farm _____ **arm, harm**

2. cart _____ **dart, part**

3. yard _____ **hard, lard**

4. shark _____ **bark, mark**

Visualization Strategy Circle the correct spelling for each word. Then write it on the line.

5. sharck (shark) sharke **shark** _____

6. hardun hardin (harden) **harden** _____

7. (sharp) sharpe scharp **sharp** _____

8. pert (part) purt **part** _____

Name _____ Date _____

▶Science Words

Fill in the blank with a science word from the box that best completes each sentence.

glacier climate fossils compass mammal oxygen

1. A whale is a __mammal_____.

2. Hawaii has a warm, mild __climate_____.

3. A __glacier_____ is a large mass of ice.

4. A __compass_____ tells you the direction you are going.

5. Scientists study dinosaur __fossils_____.

6. Trees give off the __oxygen_____ that we breathe.

VOCABULARY

UNIT 4 Fossils • **Lesson 3** *Dinosaur Fossils*

▶ Linking and Helping Verb Tenses

The present tense of a verb tells what is happening now. The past tense tells what has already happened.

▶ **Underline the linking or helping verb. Write past or present on the line.**

1. Baseball <u>is</u> played in a stadium. **present** _____

2. It <u>is</u> played on a diamond. **present** _____

3. Yesterday <u>was</u> the first game of the World Series. **past** _____

4. The Los Angeles Dodgers <u>are</u> my favorite team. **present** _____

▶ **Rewrite each sentence below. Change the verb tense from present tense to past tense.**

5. The World Series is played in October.

   The World Series was played in October. _____

6. The New York Yankees are the home team.

   The New York Yankees were the home team. _____

7. The pitcher is the best player.

   The pitcher was the best player. _____

▶Figurative Language

Figures of speech are used to create pictures in a reader's mind.

Fill in the blanks to complete the sentence.

When I woke up this morning, I saw that my alarm

had not gone off. My eyelids felt as heavy as

__Answers will vary__. I finally got up and walked to

the closet. My closet was as cluttered as

__Answers will vary__. I looked down and saw a door

that was as small as __Answers will vary__. When I

looked closer, the door was like __Answers will vary.__

WRITER'S CRAFT

▶The /er/ and /or/ Sounds

SPELLING

Proofreading Strategy Circle the words that are spelled wrong in each sentence. Then write the misspelled words correctly on the lines.

1. Would you like some (moor) pizza? **more** _____

2. Todd built a giant model of a (dinosor) **dinosaur** _____

3. The sleeves are too (shourt) **short** _____

4. We wrote a poem (fore) homework. **for** _____

Visualization Strategy Write the correct spelling for each word.

5. furst   **first** _____

6. gerl   **girl** _____

7. hert   **hurt** _____

8. swurl   **swirl** _____

9. tern   **turn** _____

▶Antonyms

▶Write a word on the line that is an antonym for each word. Then use it in a sentence.

1. hurry   slow; Answers will vary.

2. all   none; Answers will vary.

3. moist   dry; Answers will vary.

4. take   give; Answers will vary.

5. hard   soft or easy; Answers will vary.

▶Write two words that mean the opposite of each word below.

6. hot   cold, freezing, frigid

7. clean   dirty, messy

8. cry   laugh, giggle, chuckle

VOCABULARY

▶ Nouns: Singular and Plural

GRAMMAR AND USAGE

A **singular noun** names one person, place, or thing. A **plural noun** names more than one person, place, or thing.

Rewrite each of the following sentences changing the underlined singular noun into a plural noun. Remember that the subject and the verb must agree.

1. I saw a <u>butterfly</u> in the yard.

I saw butterflies in the yard.

2. I liked the <u>story</u> my dad told me.

I liked the stories my dad told me.

3. Is your <u>foot</u> cold?

Are your feet cold?

4. Did you see the <u>mouse</u>?

Did you see the mice?

5. The <u>pizza</u> for lunch was tasty.

The pizzas for lunch were tasty.

6. The <u>child</u> was wearing a uniform.

The children were wearing uniforms.

Nouns: Singular and Plural • **Challenge**

▶Organizing Descriptive Writing

How to organize your paragraph:

▶ Start with your topic.

▶ Add descriptive details.

▶ Sum up your main points at the end.

Write a paragraph describing yourself. Pretend you are writing to someone who has never met you. Be sure to use descriptive words.

Answers will vary. _____

_____

_____

_____

_____

WRITER'S CRAFT

WRITER'S CRAFT

▶ Collecting and Organizing Data

▶ You can find data in an **atlas,** a **dictionary,** an **encyclopedia, magazines** and **newspapers,** and at a **museum** or **zoo.**

▶ You can organize data using a **chart** or **time line.**

Think of something you have always wanted to know more about. It could be a planet, an animal, a country, or your city. Then write a short paragraph telling your subject, why you want to write about it, where you would find the data you need, and how you would organize the data.

Answers will vary.

_____

_____

_____

_____

▶Sequence

The writers and artists who create comic strips use both words and drawings to tell the sequence of events in their comic strips. Sometimes drawings without words tell the story.

▶**Look at several comic strips from a newspaper. Notice how writers use words in balloons to show what the characters are thinking or saying. Notice also how artists use different facial expressions and action lines to show movement.**

▶**Think about your favorite comic strip and what you like about it. Then, in the three boxes below, create your own comic strip. Use words and drawings—or drawings alone—to tell the sequence of events. Check with your teacher about sharing your comic strip with the class. Answers will vary.**

COMPREHENSION

▶ Words with *br* and *fr*

 Visualization Strategy Add *br* or *fr* to each word to complete the sentence.

1. The _____fr_____ isky cat swatted the yarn.

2. I like French _____br_____ ead.

3. Sammy is my best _____fr_____ iend.

4. The stars are _____br_____ ight tonight.

Circle the correct spelling of each word. Then write it on the line.

5. fea   freigh   (free)   free _____

6. frogg   (frog)   froug   frog _____

7. (brush)   brusch   bruch   brush _____

8. frount   fronte   (front)   front _____

9. brich   (brick)   bricke   brick _____

SPELLING

▶Analogies

▶**Fill in the blank to complete each analogy.**

1. Paw is to dog as **fin** _____ is to fish.

2. **Wrist** _____ is to hand as ankle is to foot.

3. Library is to **books** _____ as drawer is to socks.

4. Tired is to sleep as hungry is to **eat** _____.

5. Glass is to **break** _____ as cookie is to crumble.

▶**Write two analogies of your own below.**

Answers will vary.
_____

_____

VOCABULARY

GRAMMAR AND USAGE

►Adverbs

Adverbs are words that describe verbs. Adverbs can tell *when*, *where*, or *how*. Adverbs often end in *-ly*, but not always.

►**Write an adverb to complete each sentence.**

Answers will vary.

1. The dog ran _____ to the fence.

2. Stephen will arrive _____.

3. Susan left _____ I did.

4. The dog will _____ stay close to his master.

5. Patrick can swim _____.

►**Write a sentence with the adverb.**

6. quietly _____

_____

7. fast _____

_____

8. today _____

_____

▶Paragraph Form

<u>Paragraph Rules</u>

▸ Begin on a new line

▸ Indent the first line

▸ Have a topic sentence

▸ Have supporting details

Think of your favorite food. Write a paragraph about it.

Answers will vary.

_____

_____

_____

_____

_____

►**Review**

Rhyming Word Strategy
Write the spelling word that rhymes with each word.

1. rock   **shock** _____

2. beach   **reach** _____

3. wish   **fish** _____

4. bird   **third** _____

Visualization Strategy
Circle the correct spelling of each word. Then write it on the line.

5. (ever)   evir   evur   **ever** _____

6. fith   fithe   (fifth)   **fifth** _____

7. fourmed   (formed)   furmed   **formed** _____

8. chace   (chase)   shase   **chase** _____

9. (white)   whit   wite   **white** _____

▶Review

▶**Write whether each sentence uses synonyms, antonyms, or analogies.**

1. The dog's belly is fat, but his legs are skinny.

antonyms

2. Dinner is to night as breakfast is to morning.

analogies

3. The movie made us laugh and cry.

antonyms

4. The weather was cold and frigid.

synonyms

5. Book is to read as food is to eat.

analogies

6. The animal's skin was rough and coarse.

synonyms

VOCABULARY

Name _____ Date _____

▶Review

▶**Read the following sentences. Underline the adjectives and circle the adverbs.**

1. Shannon left (early) (yesterday) on a large plane.

2. She was flying (directly) to Paris, France.

▶**Rewrite each sentence. Use a contraction where possible.**

3. I have been to the Eiffel Tower.

   I've been to the Eiffel Tower.

4. My parents said we are going to visit Paris.

   My parents said we're going to visit Paris.

▶**Rewrite the sentence. Change the verb tense from past to present. Change the subject noun from singular to plural.**

5. The boy was going to take a vacation.

   The boys are going to take a vacation.

▶Topic Sentences

A topic sentence tells the main idea of a paragraph.
It is often the first sentence of a paragraph.

**Think of something you did in the summer.
Write a topic sentence and three details
about it.**

Topic Sentence: **Answers will vary.**

_____

Detail: **Answers will vary.**

Detail: **Answers will vary.**

Detail: **Answers will vary.**

WRITER'S CRAFT

UNIT 5 Courage • **Lesson I** *Molly the Brave and Me*

COMPREHENSION

▶ Point of View

▶ Write a paragraph about a true adventure that you have had. This may be an adventure in which you were brave or in which a friend was brave. You can write it from the first-person point of view or the third-person point of view. **Answers will vary.**

▶ Point of view I will use: (circle one) first person/third person

_____

_____

_____

_____

_____

_____

_____

_____

_____

_____

_____

UNIT 5 Courage • **Lesson I** *Molly the Brave and Me*

▶Words Ending in -ed and -ing

 Conventions Strategy Add *-ing* to each word. Then write a sentence using each new word to show something that is happening now. Remember to double the final consonant.

1. bat   batting   Answers will vary.

2. hit   hitting   Answers will vary.

3. run   running   Answers will vary.

4. skip   skipping   Answers will vary.

 Meaning Strategy Fill in the blank with a word from the box that best completes each sentence.

spotted	swatted	mopped	slipped

5. Rich __mopped__ the floor for the party.

6. Janie __slipped__ on the ice.

7. We __spotted__ a deer in the woods.

8. Dad __swatted__ the fly.

SPELLING

Name _____ Date _____

►Synonyms

VOCABULARY

►Choose a word from the box that is a synonym for each word. Use each word in a sentence.

build	correct	clatter	bite	look

1. right   **correct; Answers will vary.** _____

2. chew   **bite; Answers will vary.** _____

3. make   **build; Answers will vary.** _____

4. noise   **clatter; Answers will vary.** _____

5. see   **look; Answers will vary.** _____

►Write three more pairs of synonyms below.

Answers will vary. _____

_____

_____

▶ Capitalization: I and Proper Nouns

The word *I* and **proper nouns** are always capitalized.

▶ **Proofread the following paragraph. Underline the words that should be capitalized.**

Sacajawea was a <u>native</u> <u>american</u>. She was a member of the <u>shoshone</u> tribe. She was asked by the explorers, <u>lewis</u> and <u>clark</u>, to help on their expedition. They were exploring new lands bought in the <u>louisiana</u> <u>purchase</u>. The <u>louisiana</u> <u>purchase</u> nearly doubled the size of the <u>united</u> <u>states</u>. Lewis and <u>clark</u> started traveling up the <u>missouri</u> <u>river</u>. They made it all the way to the <u>pacific</u> <u>ocean</u>. They could not have done it without the help of <u>sacajawea</u>.

▶ **Read each sentence. Underline the words that should be capitalized. Circle any word that is incorrectly capitalized.**

1. I'm going to <u>new</u> York <u>city</u> for a (Vacation).

2. We went to see the <u>statue</u> of <u>liberty</u>.

3. I liked riding on the (Subway).

4. We took a walk through Central <u>park</u>.

MECHANICS

UNIT 5 Courage • **Lesson 1** *Molly the Brave and Me*

▶ Organizing Narrative Writing

WRITER'S CRAFT

Narrative writing tells a story.

Write a paragraph telling about a time you took a trip.

Answers will vary.

_____

_____

_____

_____

_____

_____

_____

UNIT 5 Courage • **Lesson 2** *Dragons and Giants*

▶ Present Tense of Words

 Visualization Strategy Write the correct spelling of each word. Then write a sentence using each word.

1. fite   **fight**
_____

Answers will vary.
_____

2. git   **get**
_____

Answers will vary.
_____

3. slyde   **slide**
_____

Answers will vary.
_____

4. giv   **give**
_____

Answers will vary.
_____

 Proofreading Strategy Circle the word that is spelled wrong in each sentence. Then write the misspelled words correctly on the lines.

5. Never (tel) a lie. **tell** _____

6. Do you (no) all the state capitals? **know** _____

7. Please help me (luk) for my notebook. **look** _____

8. Will you (driv) us there? **drive** _____

SPELLING

UNIT 5 Courage • **Lesson 2** *Dragons and Giants*

▶Antonyms

▶Draw a line from the words on the left to their antonyms on the right.

1. polite   wake

2. sleep   stale

3. sharp   sweet

4. fresh   rude

5. sour   rise

6. sink   dull

▶Write an antonym for each word below and use it in a sentence.   Answers will vary.

7. tight __loose_____   _____

8. lie __truth_____   _____

9. heavy __light_____   _____

UNIT 5 Courage • **Lesson 2** *Dragons and Giants*

▶ Conjunctions and Interjections

Conjunctions are words that connect or join phrases, words, ideas, or clauses. An **interjection** is a word that shows strong feeling or emotions.

▶ **Read the following paragraph. Add exclamation points (!) after the interjections. Underline the conjunctions.**

Jamal <u>and</u> Brett went to Scotland. Scotland is on an island with England <u>and</u> Wales. They visited Loch Ness. A loch is a lake <u>or</u> a big pond. They were eating sandwiches <u>and</u> pretzels for lunch. Then Jamal said, "Look!I see a monster." Brett said, "No way!I didn't see anything." "Yes, I'm sure," said Jamal. They looked <u>and</u> looked, <u>but</u> never saw it again.

▶ **Write a sentence using the following interjections and conjunctions.**

1. Wow! and

   _____

2. Great! but

   _____

GRAMMAR AND USAGE

UNIT 5 Courage • **Lesson 2** *Dragons and Giants*

▶Plot

WRITER'S CRAFT

A story's **plot** is the things that happen in the story.

Write a paragraph about your favorite book. Write about what happened in the story.

Answers will vary. _____

_____

_____

_____

_____

▶Suspense and Surprise

▶**Suspense** makes the reader want to find out what happens next.

▶**Surprise** is when something happens that the reader didn't expect.

Imagine you have discovered a new planet. How could you add suspense and surprise to a story you might write about this new planet?

Answers will vary.

_____

_____

_____

_____

WRITER'S CRAFT

COMPREHENSION

▶ Cause and Effect

Find the effect that best matches each cause. Draw a line between each match. Then, write the cause and effect as a joke. Check with your teacher about sharing the jokes with your class.

Cause	Effect
He was a little horse.	The man threw a stick of butter out the window.
He wanted to see a butterfly.	The pony couldn't sing.
All the fans have left.	It gets hot after a baseball game.

1. **Why couldn't the pony sing? He was a little horse.**

   _____

2. **Why did the man throw a stick of butter out the window?**

   He wanted to see a butterfly.

3. **Why does it get hot after a baseball game?**

   All the fans have left.

▶Past Tense of Words

Meaning Strategy Change each word to the past tense.

1. drive ___drove___

2. tell ___told___

3. slide ___slid___

4. come ___came___

5. live ___lived___

▶**Fill in the blank with a word from the box that best completes each sentence.**

sang	gave	looked	was

6. We ___looked___ all over for the keys.

7. She ___gave___ me a nice gift.

8. Our grandparents ___sang___ songs to us.

9. Emma ___was___ the first person in line.

SPELLING

▶Base Word Families

VOCABULARY

▶For each word below, write two other words that belong to its family. **Answers will vary.**

1. sing   singing, sings, sang _____

2. lock   relock, unlock, locked, locking _____

3. wish   wished, wishing, wishful _____

4. loose   loosen, looser _____

5. do   redo, undo, does, done _____

6. soft   soften, softly _____

▶**Write a word family of your own.** **Answers will vary.**

_____

_____

_____

▶Commas in Dialogue

Commas are used to separate quotation marks from the speaker tag and the rest of the sentence.

Rewrite the following sentences using the correct punctuation. Remember to use commas and quotation marks.

1. I'm Amber the girl said.

   "I'm Amber," the girl said.

   _____

2. My name is Anna the new girl answered.

   "My name is Anna," the new girl answered.

   _____

3. Do you like to read? Amber asked.

   "Do you like to read?" Amber asked.

   _____

4. Yes! My favorite book is <u>The Hole in the Dike</u> exclaimed Anna.

   "Yes! My favorite book is <u>The Hole in the Dike</u>," exclaimed

   Anna.

MECHANICS

UNIT 5 Courage • **Lesson 3** *The Hole in the Dike*

WRITER'S CRAFT

▶Characterization

Characterization is the writer's way of showing what the characters in a story are like.

You can make your story characters seem real to your readers. Write one or two sentences to tell what each character below does, says, thinks, or feels.

1. Chris is sad.

Answers will vary.

_____

2. Sara is funny.

Answers will vary.

_____

3. Kyle is excited.

Answers will vary.

_____

4. Hanna is nice.

Answers will vary.

_____

▶Setting

The **setting** tells the time and place in which the story happens.

Think of your favorite place to go or your favorite thing to do. Write a paragraph telling about the setting.

Answers will vary.
_____

_____

_____

_____

UNIT 5 Courage • **Lesson 4** *A Picture Book of Martin Luther King, Jr.*

▶Plurals

 Conventions Strategy Add *-s* or *-es* to each word to make a spelling word.

1. year   **years** _____

2. march   **marches** _____

3. duck   **ducks** _____

4. cow   **cows** _____

5. wash   **washes** _____

 Proofreading Strategy Circle the words that are spelled wrong in each sentence. Then write the words correctly on the lines.

6. That bakery makes the best (cacks) **cakes** _____

7. We saw (zebres) at the zoo. **zebras** _____

8. Mom bought new (glases) **glasses** _____

9. Dad (storz) his boat in the docks. **stores** _____

SPELLING

▶Prefixes

Add *pre-*, *re-*, *mis-*, or *dis-* to each underlined word to complete each sentence.

1. Do you **dis**____ agree with that answer?

2. Can you help me **pre**____ pare dinner?

3. I **mis**____ read the ingredients and the cake was ruined.

4. I will **re**____ heat the pizza for lunch tomorrow.

5. We **pre**____ ordered dinner so it would be ready when we got there.

6. He **mis**____ took me for someone else.

7. I had to **re**____ connect to the Internet when I was cut off.

8. Our teacher **dis**____ missed us early for the holiday.

VOCABULARY

▶Capitalization: Titles and Initials

MECHANICS

Titles used with a person's name are capitalized. **Initials** in names are also capitalized.

▶**Underline three times the letters that should be capitalized.**

1. The soldier looked for general washington.

2. Charlotte's web was written by e.b. white.

3. The book report was written by b.j. wilson.

4. The h.m.s. ohio was being steered by captain hayes.

▶**Write sentences beginning with the following titles.**

5. Mr. _Answers will vary._

_____

6. Dr. _____

_____

7. Mrs. _____

_____

▶Dialogue

Dialogue tells the reader exactly what the
characters say.

**Write a conversation between two or three
people. It could be on the telephone or in
person.**

Answers will vary. _____

_____

_____

_____

_____

_____

_____

_____

_____

_____

WRITER'S CRAFT

▶Sequence

COMPREHENSION

Unscramble each group of words and put them in the correct order to make a sentence. Then write the numbers *1–5* in the boxes beside the sentences to tell the correct order in which the events should happen. Use the story to help you put the sentences in the correct order.

took the Emperor Ping his pot empty to

Ping took his empty pot to the Emperor.

3

child gave seed a the each emperor

The emperor gave each child a seed.

1

Emperor new chose be the Ping Emperor
old to the

The old Emperor chose Ping to be the new Emperor.

4

seed Ping grow his could to get not

Ping could not get his seed to grow.

2

▶Suffixes

Conventions Strategy Add -*er* to each word to make a spelling word. Then use it in a sentence that compares two things. Remember to double the final consonant and change the *y* to *i* in some words.

1. slow ___slower_____

___Sentences will vary._____

2. big ___bigger_____

___Sentences will vary._____

3. silly ___sillier_____

___Sentences will vary._____

Meaning Strategy Fill in the blank with the word that best completes each sentence.

happier happiest higher highest slower slowest

4. He could jump ___higher_____ than his older brother.

5. He was the ___happiest_____ puppy of the litter.

6. My turtle moves ___slower_____ than that caterpillar.

SPELLING

▶Suffixes

▶Replace each set of underlined words with a word ending in *-er* or *-est*. Write the word on the line.

1. She is <u>more kind</u> than her sister. kinder _____

2. He is the <u>most silly</u> of all the dads. silliest _____

3. Emma is <u>more witty</u> than Sharon. wittier _____

4. The sky is <u>more clear</u> today than yesterday. clearer _____

5. He is the <u>most funny</u>. funniest _____

▶Write one sentence using a word ending in *-er* and one with a word ending in *-est*.

Answers will vary. _____

_____

_____

_____

VOCABULARY

▶ Apostrophes and Colons

An **apostrophe** is used in contractions and possessives. A **colon** is used to introduce a list of items and when telling the time.

Rewrite the following sentences using the correct punctuation. Remember to use apostrophes and colons.

1. Brittneys flight is leaving at 400.

Brittney's flight is leaving at 4:00.

_____

2. The airlines next flight wont leave until 700.

The airline's next flight won't leave until 7:00.

_____

3. She needs to pack these items shirt, pants, socks, and shoes.

She needs to pack these items: shirt, pants, socks, and

shoes.

_____

MECHANICS

UNIT 5 Courage • **Lesson 5** *The Empty Pot*

WRITER'S CRAFT

▶Sentence Combining

Two sentences with ideas that are alike can be put together, or combined by using the word *and.*

Write two sentences about each topic. Then combine them.

Topic: Your state.
Answers will vary.

_____

_____

_____

Topic: A family member.
Answers will vary.

_____

_____

_____

Sentence Combining • **Challenge**

Author's Purpose

Authors write for different reasons. They write to inform, to explain how to do something, to persuade, and to entertain. Have you ever done anything that you did not think you could do? How did you feel when you accomplished it? What did other people think? Write a story about your accomplishment.

Write the purpose for writing your story before you begin. You may choose to write to entertain, to inform your reader, or explain how you achieved your accomplishment. Answers will vary.

My purpose: _____

Title: _____

_____

_____

_____

_____

_____

_____

COMPREHENSION

UNIT 5 Courage • **Lesson 6** *Brave as a Mountain Lion*

▶Review

Visualization Strategy Circle the correct spelling for each word. Then write it on the line.

SPELLING

1. uncals   (uncles)   unclus   <u>uncles</u>

2. (tapped)   taepd   tappd   <u>tapped</u>

3. droppin   (dropping)   droping   <u>dropping</u>

4. walles   whalus   (whales)   <u>whales</u>

5. (rabbits)   rabbitz   rabits   <u>rabbits</u>

Proofreading Strategy Circle the words that are spelled wrong in each sentence. Then write the misspelled words correctly.

6. Kim's (ents) all live in different states. <u>aunts</u>

7. I want to study (animels). <u>animals</u>

8. Have you (paked) your suitcase yet? <u>packed</u>

9. My mom is the (bravist) person I know. <u>bravest</u>

Name _____ Date _____

▶Review

Make as many words as you can by adding the prefixes and suffixes from the box to each base word.

Answers will vary.

pre- re- mis- dis- -er -est

1. take   retake, mistake

2. lively   livelier, liveliest

3. count   recount, miscount, discount, counter

4. sunny   sunnier, sunniest

5. train   retrain, trainer

6. believe   disbelieve, believer

7. heat   reheat, preheat, heater

VOCABULARY

GRAMMAR, USAGE, AND MECHANICS

▶Review

▶**Underline the conjunctions in the following sentences.**

1. Transportation is a way of moving people <u>or</u> goods from one place to another.

2. Charles has a skateboard <u>and</u> a bike.

▶**Rewrite the following sentences. Add correct punctuation.**

3. "For transportation my family uses bikes scooters cars and the subway to get around" said Joel.

   "For transportation my family uses: bikes, scooters,

   cars, and the subway to get around," said Joel.

4. "My grandfather came to the united states from japan on a boat" said dr. nomo.

   "My grandfather came to the United States from

   Japan on a boat," said Dr. Nomo.

5. Oh my Were late for the 315 bus.

   Oh my! We're late for the 3:15 bus.

Name _____ Date _____

▶Time and Order Words

Time words tell when something happens.
Order words tell the order in which things
happen.

**Write a paragraph about ways you can help
nature by recycling. Be sure to use time and
order words.**

Answers will vary.

_____

_____

_____

_____

WRITER'S CRAFT

▶Prefixes

 Meaning Strategy Add *un-* or *re-* to the underlined word to complete each sentence.

1. My teacher let me <u>re</u> <u>take</u> the test.

2. Did you <u>un</u> <u>pack</u> your suitcase yet?

3. I am <u>un</u> <u>sure</u> about what I will do.

 Visualization Strategy Write the correct spelling for each word. Then use each word in a sentence of your own.

4. ineven <u>**uneven**</u>

Answers will vary

5. reetest <u>**retest**</u>

Answers will vary

6. unlocke <u>**unlock**</u>

Answers will vary

7. riname <u>**rename**</u>

Answers will vary

▶Social Studies Words

Fill in the blank with a social studies word from the box that best completes each sentence.

astronaut capital freedom traded country election

1. Before they used money, people __traded__ goods.

2. The Civil War was fought to give slaves __freedom__.

3. Neil Armstrong was the first __astronaut__ to walk on the moon.

4. The United States is a free __country__.

5. We have an __election__ to vote for the president.

6. The __capital__ of Hawaii is Honolulu.

VOCABULARY

▶Review

Proofread the paragraph. Underline words that should be capitalized three times (≡). Cross out any possessive noun or pronoun that is used incorrectly. Write the correct word above it.

o̲rville and w̲ilber w̲right were the first

They
people to fly an airplane. ~~Them~~ were born in

d̲ayton, o̲hio. Before making an airplane the

brothers   **people**
w̲right ~~brothers'~~ made bikes. Many ~~peoples~~

didn't think that an airplane was possible. The

their
w̲right brothers worked hard to make ~~they're~~

Their
plane. ~~Theirs~~ first flight was in 1903 in n̲orth

c̲arolina. The first airplane's name was *Flyer*.

The first flight lasted just 12 seconds. But once

they   **they**
~~their~~ did it, ~~them~~ knew they could make better

airplanes They
~~airplane's.~~ ~~Them~~ made many planes after the

first one.

►Audience and Purpose

Your **audience** is your reader.

Your **purpose** is your reason for writing.

Tell the audience and purpose of this paragraph.

    <u>Amelia Bedelia</u> is a funny book. Amelia is a good cook, but she gets things mixed up. You never know what she'll do. She even takes some light bulbs outside and hangs them on a clothesline! I think you will enjoy this book.

Purpose: <u>**to persuade someone to read this book**</u>

Audience: <u>**friends, classmates, family**</u>

▶Cause and Effect

Look in "New Hope." Find sentences in which the author tells about an event. Look in the story for the cause of the event. Write the event and the cause.

Answers will vary. Possible answers are shown.

Event: **Jimmy loved to visit Grandpa.**

_____

_____

Cause: **He loved the old-fashioned ice-cream store in**

New Hope, where Grandpa lived. He loved the recycling

dump. And he especially loved the statue in the park.

Event: **New Hope became a busy, bustling place.**

_____

_____

Cause: **As the years passed, more and more people came**

to the village by the river.

▶ Suffixes

 Conventions Strategy Add *-ful* or *-less* to each underlined word to complete each sentence.

1. The broken flashlight was <u>use</u> **less** _____.

2. We had a <u>wonder</u> **ful** _____ time at the party!

3. I felt <u>help</u> **less** _____ when I broke my leg.

4. The <u>play</u> **ful** _____ puppy licked our faces.

 Rhyming Strategy Write the base of a spelling word that rhymes with each word. Then add *-ful* or *-less* to it to make a spelling word. The first one is done for you.

5. cob   job   jobless

6. grape   **shape** _____   **shapeless** _____

7. farm   **harm** _____   **harmful or harmless** _____

8. blue   **clue** _____   **clueless** _____

9. rope   **hope** _____   **hopeful or hopeless** _____

SPELLING

UNIT 6 Our Country and Its People • **Lesson 2** *New Hope*

▶Suffixes

VOCABULARY

▶**Replace the underlined words with a word ending in -ful or -less.**

1. The sky was <u>without stars</u>. starless _____

2. We were <u>full of hope</u>. hopeful _____

3. The firefighter was <u>without fear</u>. fearless _____

4. She was <u>full of cheer</u>. cheerful _____

5. The poor dog was <u>without a home</u>. homeless _____

▶**Write two sentences using words ending in -ful and -less.**   **Answers will vary.**

_____

_____

▶Review

▶**Proofread the letter. Underline three times any letter (≡) that should be capitalized. Add quotation marks and commas where they should be.**

d̲ear Dave,

i̲ hope you will be able to visit me on

s̲aturday, j̲uly 10, 2002. w̲e will be able to go to

the swimming pool, the park, the zoo, and maybe

the library. My mom says, "If you get an early

start, you should be able to do it all." h̲ave you

read the book <u>Arthur's Computer Disaster</u>? It's

one of my favorites. I'll see you at school on

m̲onday.

y̲our friend,

Sean

MECHANICS

WRITER'S CRAFT

▶ Words of Request

Words of request help you ask for things in a nice way.

Pretend you have to write a report on dinosaurs for school. Write a short letter to someone at a museum asking for information on dinosaurs. Make sure your words are polite.

Answers will vary. _____

_____

_____

_____

_____

_____

_____

▶Compound Words

 Compound Word Strategy Draw a line from the words on the left to the words on the right to make a spelling word. Write the words on the lines.

1. no   one   <u>**nobody**</u>

2. in   self   <u>**inside**</u>

3. every   body   <u>**everyone**</u>

4. sun   room   <u>**sunrise**</u>

5. lunch   side   <u>**lunchroom**</u>

6. my   rise   <u>**myself**</u>

 Meaning Strategy Make up two compound words and use them each in a sentence.

7. <u>**Answers will vary.**</u>

8. <u>**Answers will vary.**</u>

SPELLING

▶ Compound Words

VOCABULARY

▶ **Add a word from the box to the front and back of each base word below to make two new compound words. Write the words on the line.**

field	in	mark	dug	house
left	sun	knob	note	board

1. light __sunlight, lighthouse__

2. book __notebook, bookmark__

3. over __leftover, overboard__

4. door __indoor, doorknob__

5. out __dugout, outfield__

▶ **Write two more sentences using compound words.**

__Answers will vary__

_____

Name _____ Date _____

 # Review

▶ Write *declarative, interrogative, imperative,* or *exclamatory* on the line. Underline the subject and circle the predicate.

1. Thomas Edison (was born in Milan, Ohio, in 1837.)

   declarative

2. Thomas Edison (invented the light bulb.)

   declarative

3. He (must have been really smart!) exclamatory

4. (Would) you (please invent something?)

   imperative

▶ Rewrite the run-on sentence correctly as two sentences. In the new sentences underline the linking or helping verbs.

5. Thomas Edison was an inventor he was a very

   hard worker. Thomas Edison <u>was</u> an inventor. He <u>was</u> a

   very hard worker.

GRAMMAR AND USAGE

▶ Structure of Scripts

A **script** is a group of sentences that tells people what to do and say.

Write a short script about three people lost in the woods. Write the characters' names and add stage directions.

Answers will vary.

_____

_____

_____

_____

_____

_____

_____

WRITER'S CRAFT

UNIT 6   Our Country and Its People • **Lesson 4** *The Story of the Statue of Liberty*

▶Homophones

 Meaning Strategy Write a sentence using the words below.

1. meet ___**Answers will vary.**_____

2. two ___**Answers will vary.**_____

3. sea ___**Answers will vary.**_____

4. rode ___**Answers will vary.**_____

Replace the underlined word with the spelling word that best completes each sentence.

5. May I have a <u>peace</u> of notebook paper? **piece**_____

6. Let's <u>meat</u> at the store after school. **meet**_____

7. I was in the <u>forth</u> row at the concert. **fourth**_____

8. We <u>road</u> the bus to school this morning. **rode**_____

9. Whales live in the <u>see</u>. **sea**_____

SPELLING

▶Homophones

▶Finish each riddle with a pair of homophones from the box.

beet	pale	sight	banned	chilly
site	beat	pail	chili	band

VOCABULARY

1. Cold stew is <u>chilly chili</u>.

2. A white bucket is a <u>pale pail</u>.

3. A music group that is forbidden is a <u>banned band</u>.

4. A blended vegetable is a <u>beat beet</u>.

5. A place to go to see is a <u>sight site</u>.

▶Write two pairs of homophones and use them in a sentence.

Answers will vary.

_____

_____

UNIT 6 **Our Country and Its People • Lesson 4** *The Story of the Statue of Liberty*

▶Review

▶ **Write an adjective for each noun. Then write a sentence using the adjective and the noun.**

1. _____ computer   **Answers will vary.**

   _____

2. _____ house

   _____

▶ **Write a sentence using the adverb.**   **Answers will vary.**

3. yesterday _____

   _____

4. often _____

   _____

▶ **Write a sentence using a contraction of the two words given.**   **Answers will vary.**

5. she will _____

   _____

GRAMMAR AND USAGE

▶ Making Inferences

COMPREHENSION

▶ Each sentence suggests a place. Read each sentence. On the line write the letter of the place that is suggested by the sentence.

a. grocery store **b.** playground **c.** library **d.** museum

b _____ **1.** Molly slid down the slide and played on the swings.

d _____ **2.** We saw a dinosaur skeleton.

a _____ **3.** Jeff paid for the milk, eggs, and bread.

c _____ **4.** We sat in a circle for storytime.

▶ Choose one of the places listed above. Write three sentences describing that place, but don't tell what it is. When you are finished, ask a partner to read your paragraph and guess which place you wrote about.

Answers will vary.

_____

_____

_____

_____

▶ Homographs

 Meaning Strategy Write two sentences using each word below in a different way.

Answers will vary.

1. lead _____

_____

2. wind _____

_____

3. dove _____

_____

For each underlined word, write a sentence using the other meaning of the word.

4. My uncle has a <u>sow</u> on his farm.

Answers will vary.

_____

5. He got a lot of <u>presents</u> for his birthday.

Answers will vary.

_____

6. Be sure to <u>close</u> the gate when you leave.

Answers will vary.

_____

SPELLING

▶ Homographs

VOCABULARY

**Write two sentences for each word. Be sure to use a
different meaning for each sentence.   Answers will vary**

1. bow _____

_____

2. dove _____

_____

3. live _____

_____

4. sewer _____

_____

5. tear _____

_____

▶Review

▶Rewrite the sentence changing the verb tense from past to present. Underline the helping or linking verb in the sentence you write.

1. The koala bears were living in Australia.

   The koala bears <u>are</u> living in Australia.

▶Read the sentence. The verb is underlined. Write *helping* or *linking* on the first line. On the second line write *past* or *present*.

2. Australia <u>is</u> a large island in the Pacific Ocean.

   linking _____   **present** _____

▶Write the plural form of the singular noun. Then write a sentence using the plural noun. Plural shown.
                                                    Answer will vary.

3. bunny **bunnies** _____

   _____

GRAMMAR AND USAGE

WRITER'S CRAFT

▶ Words of Request

Words of request help you ask for things in a nice way.

Pretend you bought a computer that doesn't work. Write a letter to someone at the computer company asking for help or a new computer. Make sure your words are polite.

Answers will vary. _____

_____

_____

_____

_____

_____

_____

UNIT 6 Our Country and Its People • **Lesson 6** *A Piece of Home*

▶Words with Foreign Origins

Foreign Language Strategy Write the spelling words that end with the same sound as each word below.

1. mellow _pinto, burro, bronco_

2. hay _buffet, beret, ballet_

Visualization Strategy Circle the correct spelling of each spelling word. Then write it on the line.

SPELLING

3. buroe   buro   (burro)   _burro_

4. (siesta)   seista   seasta   _siesta_

5. pretsel   prezel   (pretzel)   _pretzel_

6. buffay   (buffet)   bufett   _buffet_

7. feista   feasta   (fiesta)   _fiesta_

► **Multicultural Words**

VOCABULARY

Use each multicultural word in a sentence.

1. cheetah **Answers will vary.** _____

2. trophy **Answers will vary.** _____

3. chef **Answers will vary.** _____

4. tornado **Answers will vary.** _____

5. loaf **Answers will vary.** _____

6. piano **Answers will vary.** _____

List multicultural words of your own in the space below.

_____

_____

_____

_____

_____

_____

Name _____ Date _____

▶Review

▶ **Underline the interjections and conjunctions in the following sentences.**

1. "Oh no! I forgot my scooter <u>and</u> my bike," said Rasheed.

2. Holly exclaimed, "<u>Yes</u>! I got an A on my math test <u>and</u> my spelling test."

▶ **Rewrite the following sentences. Add correct punctuation.**

3. "To make a good sandwich you need bread lettuce tomatoes, and pickles" said mrs. henderson.

   "To make a good sandwich you need: bread, lettuce,

   tomatoes, and pickles," said Mrs. Henderson.

   _____

4. "my grandmother from germany makes the best sandwiches" said Kathy.

   "My grandmother from Germany makes the best

   sandwiches," said Kathy.

   _____

GRAMMAR, USAGE AND MECHANICS

WRITER'S CRAFT

▶ Supporting Details

Supporting details tell about the main idea.

Write a paragraph about the main idea below. Use at least three details to support the main idea.

Main Idea: Everyone should know how to read and write.

Answers will vary. _____

_____

_____

_____

_____

UNIT 6 Our Country and its People • **Lesson 7** *Jalapeño Bagels*

▶Fact and Opinion

Think of a food you enjoy. Look at a cookbook or an encyclopedia to find some facts about the food. Write a paragraph including some of the facts you discovered and some opinions you have about the food.

Answers will vary.

_____

_____

_____

_____

_____

_____

_____

_____

_____

_____

_____

_____

_____

COMPREHENSION

▶ Review

SPELLING

 Compound Word Strategy Change the second word in each compound word to make a spelling word. Write the new word on the line.

1. someone   **something**

2. turnout   **turnovers**

3. noteworthy   **notebook**

4. everybody   **everything**

5. inside   **into**

 Meaning Strategy Fill in the blank with a word from the box that best completes each sentence.

whatever	forth	four	peace

6. Dad changed all _____**four**_____ tires on our car.

7. We go to the country for _____**peace**_____ and relaxation.

8. She drove back and _____**forth**_____ for an hour to find a parking place.

9. _____**Whatever**_____ you do, don't go near that alligator!

Name _____ Date _____

▶Review

▶**Write a homophone for each word.**

1. won   <u>one</u>

2. dear   <u>deer</u>

3. sell   <u>cell</u>

4. its   <u>it's</u>

5. cent   <u>sent or scent</u>

▶**Choose a multicultural word from the box that best completes each sentence.**

yogurt	cola	essay	taco

6. We wrote an <u>essay</u> for English class.

7. Sometimes I drink a <u>cola</u> with lunch.

8. I had a <u>taco</u> for dinner last night.

9. Mom gave us <u>yogurt</u> for dessert.

VOCABULARY

Name _____ Date _____

▶Review

GRAMMAR AND USAGE

▶ Read the paragraph. Use the adjectives and adverbs in the box to fill in the blank spaces. **Answers may vary. Possible answers shown.**

softly	happily	three	quickly	wooden
patiently	new	roller	rapidly	wide

Todd, Doug, Howard, and their dad walked

__happily__ down the __wide__ road. The

__three__ brothers had been waiting

__patiently__ all week to go to the __new__

carnival that was in town. Todd decided to ride

the Ferris wheel and spin __quickly__ around

and around. Doug wanted to ride the carousel

and listen to the music play __softly__ as the

__wooden__ horses went up and down. Howard

chose to ride the __roller__ coaster because

he wanted to feel the wind blow __rapidly__

past his face as the cars sped along the track.

▶Plagiarism

Make sure you write papers in your own words.

Rewrite this paragraph in your own words.

The nervous system is made up of the brain, the spinal cord, and nerves. It lets us think, see, hear, move, and feel. The nerves are in the spinal cord. They carry data from the brain to the rest of the body. The brain tells us how to think and act.

Answers will vary.

_____

_____

_____

_____

WRITER'S CRAFT